Mary Magdalene: The Life and Legacy of the Woman Who Witnessed the
Crucifixion and Resurrection of Jesus

By Gustavo Vázquez Lozano & Charles River Editors

*The Penitent Mary Magdalene* by Domenico Tintoretto

## About Charles River Editors

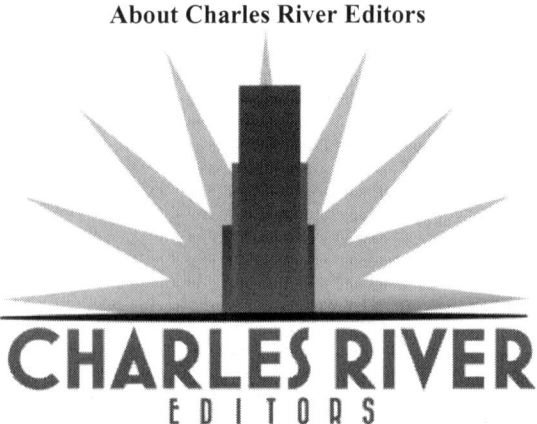

**Charles River Editors** is a boutique digital publishing company, specializing in bringing history back to life with educational and engaging books on a wide range of topics. Keep up to date with our new and free offerings with this 5 second sign up on our weekly mailing list, and visit Our Kindle Author Page to see other recently published Kindle titles.

We make these books for you and always want to know our readers' opinions, so we encourage you to leave reviews and look forward to publishing new and exciting titles each week.

# Introduction

**Raimond Spekking's picture of a statue depicting Mary Magdalene**

## Mary Magdalene

"After that, Jesus traveled about from one town and village to another. The Twelve were with him, and also some women who had been cured of evil spirits and diseases: Mary (called Mary Magdalene) from whom seven demons had come out—and many others. These women were helping to support them out of their own means." - Luke 8:1-3

Mary Magdalene is one of the most talked about figures in modern Christianity, a woman who mainstream media and modern sensibilities can hold with more conviction. The media, press, movie industry, and airport literature have been obsessed with this redhead for more than 100 years, a fascination that reached its climax in the first decade of this century, and does not seem likely to end any time soon. Mary Magdalene is frequently depicted as young and attractive, liberated and intelligent, a symbol of a freer spirituality, and not controlled by a male-dominated church. In the minds of many, she embodies opposition to a system dominated by old men in white cassocks, the "sacred feminine." As if that is not enough, she has the best bachelor in the world: Jesus Christ himself.

The French-made, fair-haired Mary Magdalene who appears in innumerable works of medieval and modern art with a red robe, a symbol of rebellion and freedom (although in the Middle Ages the intention was to show her as a loose woman), is a creation of the Western Church and, more recently, the media. It is a depiction laden with centuries of intertextual struggles, patronizing homilies, medieval legends, novels looking for bestseller status, and documentaries for cable television. But there was a historical Mary Magdalene, a woman named Miriam (Hebrew for Mary) born in Galilee in the time of King Herod, and she died, most likely in present-day Turkey, when Christianity was only a variant of Judaism. Mary Magdalene would not recognize herself in modern portraits or the perception the average Christian of the last 1500 years has of her. If there has been a search for the historical Jesus since the 18th century, the real man who walked in the hills of Galilee and died on a cross in Jerusalem, a similar quest is necessary for the historical Mary Magdalene, but not out of mere curiosity, because she is important in the narrative of Jesus's life. If the early sources are accurate, Mary of Magdala was the first Christian in history, and the first to announce the fundamental kerygma of early Christianity: Jesus is risen!

**An icon of St. Mary Magdalene with the Greek words "Christ Is Risen"**

Despite the shortage of information, there are a few certain facts historians know about Mary Magdalene. For example, she was a respected and well-remembered follower of Jesus, one of the female disciples who supported the movement of the Galilean preacher. Some scholars studying the gospels believe that Mary Magdalene was an elderly woman and probably well-to-do, if not wealthy. "For all we know," opines E.P. Sanders in *The Historical Figure of Jesus*, "she was eighty-six, childless, and keen to mother unkempt young men." She not only remained by Jesus' side in his darkest hour, the crucifixion, she also had a strange experience at Jesus's tomb on Easter morning. The gospels disagree on the details, but not in the fact that it happened to her.

*Mary Magdalene: The Life and Legacy of the Woman Who Witnessed the Crucifixion and Resurrection of Jesus* examines what is known and unknown about one of the Bible's most famous figures. Along with pictures depicting important people, places, and events, you will learn about Mary Magdalene like never before.

Mary Magdalene: The Life and Legacy of the Woman Who Witnessed the Crucifixion and Resurrection of Jesus

About Charles River Editors

Introduction

   Apparition and Authority

   In Search of the Historical Mary Magdalene

   The Life of Mary Magdalene

   A Female Leader in the Early Church

   The Disappearance of Mary Magdalene

   Online Resources

   Bibliography

Free Books by Charles River Editors

Discounted Books by Charles River Editors

## Apparition and Authority

New Testament scholar John Dominic Crossan has rightly pointed out how in the early Church, apparitions of Jesus were intimately related to leadership and authority. Claiming to have had a vision of Jesus meant they were influenced and had deference for that person. Paul, the apostle, based all of his teachings on the claim he received a special apparition of the risen Jesus.

Under this perspective, the first person ever to see the risen Jesus, and the first person to preach the news, must have been an incredibly influential and authoritative person in the early Church. There are numerous indications in the sources of the first two centuries that Mary Magdalene was that person, and thus a pillar of the primitive Church. But strangely, as early as the mid-first century, Mary Magdalene's figure of special status was fading away; she was outlined as an unreliable, hysterical witness, and later a loose woman and repentant sinner. Even in the earliest gospel, Mark, a careful reader can notice the name-calling and efforts to discredit her.

Most people are curious to know whether Mary Magdalene was the wife of Jesus or had any romantic relationship with him. However, that notion is a later creation, a misreading of the early sources, and ultimately an irrelevant aspect compared to her real achievement, one which was inexplicably darkened and hidden with the passing of time: Mary Magdalene was the first Christian, and one of the most influential and authoritative figures of the first generation. Who she was, what the historical "Miriam of Migdal" did, what her message was (if any), and why her role as an apostle was deleted from history and substituted for that of a prostitute (something that is never mentioned in the gospels) are the real issues for scholars and historians to investigate and attempt to answer.

## In Search of the Historical Mary Magdalene

Mary Magdalene (Μαρία ἡ Μαγδαληνή), literally Mary the Mary Magdalene, or Mary of Magdala, was a follower of the "Jesus movement." Some scholars believe they have found evidence in the gospels indicating she was an elderly woman and probably wealthy, or at least well-off. In the New Testament, she is seen as a member of the groups of women who gave financial or material support to the wandering disciples. It's likely she was part of that group that roamed from village to village, although this is not necessarily the case. She was remembered in the early communities of Christians, or some of them, as the first person to announce that Jesus had been raised, and in some circles as the first person to see the risen Christ, clearly an outstanding honor. Mary Magdalene and Easter Morning are, in all four gospels, two indissoluble facts. Nobody in the gospel narrative has such a prominent and exalted position, with perhaps the exception of Peter "the rock," the beloved disciple. Like Peter's sobriquet, Mary Magdalene is not a name, but an epithet that means "Tower", "Great" or "Elegant." The nickname can mean that Mary was known as "Mary the Tower," or "Mary the Great," or simply that she came from a town called Magdala.

The most insurmountable problem about her historicity, capable of overthrowing the whole case, is her inexplicable absence in the earliest known Christian documents, documents even older than the Gospels: the letters of the apostle Paul. In the authentic letters of Paul, one of the most influential leaders of the first generation of Christians, readers find the first mention of a man named Jesus of Nazareth and the existence of a religious and social movement based around him, founded on the belief that he had been resurrected after his execution at the hands of the Roman authorities. No other inscription on stone, painting, archaeological evidence, papyrus or known gospel, apocryphal or not, precedes Paul's testimony.[1]

His first epistle was written around 49 CE and the rest in the following decade. Paul's authentic letters are a mine of information about the expansion of Christianity and the original leaders of the movement. He discussed the three pillars of the early Church - the apostles Peter, John, and James the brother of Jesus. Other names such as Apollo, Silvanus, Timothy, Philemon and Prisca, as well as other associates, followers, and supporters, appear in the epistles as people who contributed to the well-being of the first communities. Paul also refers to enemies, opponents, and people who preach "another gospel." (2 Cor 11:4) Unfortunately, he doesn't mention their names. Maybe Mary Magdalene (or her community) was among them.

Scholars are particularly interested in a list of people that the apostle presents in his first letter to the Corinthians. The verses show traces of being an old pre-Pauline Christian hymn with the names or affiliation of those who in the past (from Paul's point of view) were witnesses to Jesus's resurrection, that is, people who were favored with a vision of the risen Christ. "For I delivered unto you first of all that which also I received: that Christ died for our sins according to the scriptures; and that he was buried; and that he hath been raised on the third day according to the scriptures; and that he appeared to Cephas; then to the twelve; then he appeared to above five hundred brethren at once, of whom the greater part remain until now, but some are fallen asleep; then he appeared to James; then to all the apostles; and last of all, as to the child untimely born, he appeared to me also." (1 Cor 15:3-8) [2]

---

[1] There are 13 letters attributed to Paul in the New Testament, of which seven are considered authentic by the great majority of biblical scholars, while there is difference of opinions over the rest.

[2] All quotes from the Bible are from the New Revised Standard Version, Anglicised.

*Appearance of Jesus Christ to Maria Magdalena* by Alexander Andreyevich Ivanov

The pre-Pauline formula is made clear by the way the apostle finishes the list, placing his vision of Jesus as something happening out of time when the era of the apparitions had ended; in other words, he presents it as a special distinction that gave him authority to preach the gospel. If Paul wrote this letter around 55 CE, the formula dates from at least 10 years before, in the 40s CE or even earlier.

Paul alludes to several women in his epistles, including some in important positions, such as Apphia, Julia, Phoebe, and notably, one named Mary (Rom 16: 6), which may or may not be Mary Magdalene. The problem that has troubled scholars is why Paul did not mention her as part of the group who had a vision of the risen Jesus. The theories have varied; for some, Mary Magdalene is absent because the tradition of women at the tomb on Easter morning is a later creation, while others believe Paul omitted her because mentioning a woman or group of women as the first witnesses of the resurrection did not help his cause. What Paul was offering was a list of reliable witnesses who may be consulted in case of doubt, since "the greater part remain until now, but some have fallen asleep." In essence, he was saying that some were still alive, and that those reading his works could verify that for themselves. But at the time, women in Greek cities (like Corinth) "lacked many of the legal rights given to their male counterparts. They were excluded from appearing in law courts or participating in the assembly. They were also legally prohibited from engaging in contracts (and) there was an expectation that respectable women should not appear or even be talked about in public." (Pomeroy, 1994)

A woman's testimony was considered to be unconvincing, and clearly, Paul was trying to settle a controversy among the Corinthians. Under Roman law, the situation of women was not flattering either. In 195 BCE, the tribune L. Valerius wrote, "No offices (for women), *no priesthoods*, no triumphs, no spoils of war. Elegance, adornment, finery —these are a woman's insignia." 400 hundred years later, the situation was not much better, as demonstrated by what Jurist Ulpian wrote in 200 CE: "Women are barred from all civil and public functions. They may not be judges or jurors, or hold magistracies, or appear in court or intercede for others, or be agents."

Considering all this, it was not uncommon in the early years of Christianity for some observers to laugh at the fact that the first testimony of Jesus's resurrection came from a woman. A Greek philosopher named Celsus wrote a treatise titled "The True Word" (now lost), in which he tried to demonstrate the absurdity of the claims of Christianity. When he dealt with the subject of Jesus's resurrection, Celsus made fun of Mary Magdalene, writing, "And who beheld this? A half-frantic woman, as you state."

Some prominent Biblical scholars believe that Mary Magdalene's non-appearance in the oldest report means that the story of women at the empty tomb was invented by Mark, the gospel writer, when he composed his text around 65-69 CE. If so, the female disciples may have been added to the drama with some purpose that is not entirely clear now. On the other hand, the opposite could be the case; when Paul wrote his letter to the Corinthians in 55 CE, a slow but progressive tendency to eliminate women (Mary Magdalene in particular) from important roles in the Church was already taking place. Indeed, it is harder to explain why Mark, the oldest gospel, writing 10 years after Paul, would invent the story of a terrified and grief-stricken woman, in the darkness of dawn, as the first witness of the resurrection, unless that tradition had been there from the beginning.

In the 15th year of the reign of Emperor Tiberius, according to Luke (circa 30 CE), a rural man from Galilee, the mountainous area north of present-day Israel, began a movement of passive resistance whose central message was the imminent arrival of the Kingdom of God to Earth. Jesus of Nazareth talked in parables, both spoken and acted; the same when he spoke of a mustard seed becoming a huge tree in whose branches birds made their nests, and when he burst in the Temple of Jerusalem with a whip made of ropes. Every deed and word of Jesus pointed to a greater truth; his spoken and acted parables demanded an interpretation and commitment from his listeners and witnesses. "He who has ears, let him use them," and "Whoever wants to be my disciple must take up their cross and follow me" are both an invitation and a challenge to become part of the Kingdom movement.

**Carole Raddato's picture of a bust of Tiberius**

Jesus was active in a volatile political and social environment, among aspiring messiahs, bandits and revolutionaries. His parables - about seeds and fields, birds and foxes, fish catching, rain clouds and tenants waiting for his master - are all indications that his message was aimed at the peasant class, especially the dispossessed. "Blessed are the poor, blessed are they that suffer persecution for justice' sake, blessed are those who weep," he said in one of the pericopes universally recognized as authentic. The Gospels never place him in the great cities near his native Nazareth, such as Sepphoris and Tiberias, the capital of Galilee (which had a theater that could seat 7,000 people and a gymnasium), but in small and rural localities such as Chorazin, Capernaum, Nain, Bethsaida, and Gennesaret. Many of the villages mentioned were on the shores of the Sea of Galilee, also called the Lake of Gennesaret.

Mary of Magdala, presumably living over a longer period of time than Jesus, witnessed more political turmoil and violence. Judas of Galilee rebelled in 6 CE together with Zadok, a Pharisee. They headed a large number of revolutionary fighters and ravaged the countryside, attacking both the occupying authorities and Jews who collaborated with the Census mentioned by the

Gospel of Luke. Judas was a failed aspirant to Messiah - he proclaimed the Jewish state and recognized God alone as King. In 46 CE, another uprising in Galilee by the brothers Jacob and Simon broke out, lasting for two years until both were captured and executed. When Emperor Caligula ordered a statue of himself erected in the Temple of Jerusalem in 40 CE, the whole region prepared for a war of annihilation. The most disastrous war started in 66 CE, around the end of the lives of the original apostles, and it ended with the destruction of Jerusalem.

**Louis le Grand's picture of a bust of Caligula**

The times of Jesus (circa 4 BCE-30 CE) were relatively calm in comparison with what disciples like James or Mary Magdalene witnessed. The towns where Jesus preached and where his oldest base of followers materialized, those who retained their words and deeds by means of telling and retelling oral traditions, were villages of a few hundred people. They depended on agriculture and fishing, off the main trade routes and burdened by taxes.

By the very characteristics of Jesus's movement (empowering people to create a base of resistance based on the belief of the imminent arrival of the Kingdom of God), his ministry was itinerant, without a fixed base of operations or intermediaries. For this reason, the Gospels present him wandering from one town to another, first through the region of Galilee, and at the end of his ministry in Jerusalem, where he would be executed. Jesus demanded his followers not to take anything for the road and not to settle in any house. When he sent his disciples to travel through Galilee to extend the Kingdom, he told them, "Take nothing for your journey, neither staves, nor pack, neither bread, neither money; neither have two coats apiece. And whatsoever house ye enter into, there abide and thence depart." In another verse that most scholars identify as one of the earliest layers of the gospels, Jesus exclaims, presumably referring to himself, "The foxes have holes, and the birds of the air have nests, but the Son of Man hath nowhere to lay His head."

It may be difficult for modern readers to fully grasp the complex social hierarchy and the strongly defined family roles in the ancient Mediterranean. With his preference for the destitute (those who had lost their possessions and had only their hands to survive), the women, the sick, and the children, Jesus's movement was a kingdom of nobodies, or as John Dominic Crossan dubbed it, a "kingdom of undesirables." Attitudes towards children and women were very different then than at the present time. When Jesus said, "Let the little children come to me, and do not hinder them, for the kingdom of heaven belongs to such as these," he is not being nice or politically correct, like a politician trying to win votes. He is marking a line and making clear that his movement is open preferentially to the less appreciated elements of society.

Crossan exemplifies what it meant to be a child (and a female, for that matter) with a letter found in an excavation in Oxyrhynchus, Egypt, dated 1 BCE. In it, A man named Hilaron wrote to his wife, "Know that we are even yet in Alexandria. Do not worry if they all come back (except me) and I remain in Alexandria. I urge you and entreat you, be concerned about the child (our son), and if should receive my wages soon, I will send them up to you. If by chance you bear a son, if it is a boy, let it be; if it's a girl cast it out (to die)."

Women were expected to be confined at home, so a loose, independent woman was seen as a peril and even as intrinsically evil. In the "Testament of Reuben", which is part of a larger work called "Testament of the Twelve Patriarchs," whose final edition dates from the 2nd century CE, a passage states, "For evil are women, my children; and since they have no power or strength over man, they use wiles by outward attractions that they may draw him to themselves. And whom they cannot bewitch by outward attractions, him they overcome by craft. For moreover, concerning them, the angel of the Lord told me, and taught me, that women are overcome by the spirit of fornication more than men, and in their heart they plot against men; and by means of their adornment they deceive first their minds, and by the glance of the eye instil the poison, and then through the accomplished act they take them captive." (Test Reub, 5:1-4). Even more, "rabbinic literature expressed an even more stridently misogynistic attitude toward women. Women were described not only as evil temptresses, but also as witches and nymphomaniacs." (Tetlow, 1980).

It is in this atmosphere that Mary Magdalene and the rest of the women (and children) who appear in the New Testament lived. When Jesus warned the disciples that to enter the Kingdom they must be like children, he is not saying something very different than "prostitutes will get into the Kingdom of God before you." When Jesus stands before the adulterous woman that an angry crowd is about to stone to death, he is overturning all the social rules. Jesus "stands alone as a founder of a religious sect that did not discriminate against women. Jesus favored women much higher than society did. He did not simply say they were equal. He went out of his way to elevate them. He was a pioneer in crossing cultural boundaries, risking reputation and legal consequences to add incredible value to women wherever he went." (Starr, 1955).

In the Gospels, women not only appear more prominently than in other literary works of the time, they also are depicted as models of intelligence and understanding, unlike the male apostles, who are often portrayed as stubborn and hard-headed. They are also depicted as supporters, ministers, and loyal companions.

Like in the Hebrew Bible, women play prominent roles in the New Testament. In several instances, they appear as recipients of healings and are willing to receive the instruction and preaching of Jesus. Indeed, in the Gospel of John, a Samaritan woman even embarks on a theological discussion with Jesus, made all the more remarkable by the fact that in Judea, women did not attend the synagogues, could not touch the scriptures, and were not taught the Torah, a privilege reserved for men.

The Gospels clearly indicate that Jesus's movement was sympathetic toward women and that they were welcome in the public preaching. In an episode that appears in the Gospel of Matthew, Jesus is teaching when some come to tell him that his mother and brothers are looking for him. "While he was still speaking to the crowds, his mother and his brothers were standing outside, wanting to speak to him. Someone told him, 'Look, your mother and your brothers are standing outside, wanting to speak to you.' But to the one who had told him this, Jesus replied, 'Who is my mother, and who are my brothers?' And pointing to his disciples, he said, 'Here are my mother and my brothers! For whoever does the will of my Father in heaven is my brother and sister and mother.'" (Matt 12:46-50). Although the reader cannot see the crowd, Jesus's words indicate that the audience was composed of both men and women.

In the Gospel of John, when Jesus visits the house of the most famous pair of sisters in the New Testament, Mary and Martha, he exalts and praises the one who chooses to receive instruction over the sister who opts for the chores of the house. The support was mutual. Jesus's movement was ministered by female sympathizers who gave material help to itinerant preachers, including Jesus. In the Gospel of Luke Luke, several of them are mentioned traveling with the group, and some had been healed of physical or spiritual ailments.

It should not be assumed that all of them necessarily traveled with the itinerant disciples. It is possible that the majority were well-off women who remained in their homes (such as Martha and Mary of Bethany), some of them close to official circles, like Joanna, and some others possibly working anonymously.

**The Life of Mary Magdalene**

For many, it will come as a surprise to learn that, until the crucifixion, we only find one brief mention of Mary Magdalene, which is found in the Gospel of Luke (Lk 8:1-3). She does not appear again until the Golgotha, at the foot of the cross with a group of female followers.[3]

**A 14th century painting depicting Mary Magdalene kissing the feet of Jesus**

The epithet "Mary Magdalene" was so inseparably linked to her that it became a substitute name, as in Peter's case, whose real name was Simon. Although there is no consensus on the meaning of the epithet "Mary Magdalene", the majority opinion is that it refers to her hometown, which has been identified as a small fishing village called Magdala, by the Sea of Galilee. This could be the town of Taricheae, which was mentioned by the historian Flavius Josephus, although there were several Roman villages with the same name. The name Magdala, which means "Tower", may be due to the existence of an important tower where salt fish was stored. In the Talmud, the village is identified with the name of Migdal Nûnnaya ("Fish Tower"). A mention in the Jerusalem Talmud to a fishing town called Migdal Seb'aiya (Tower of Dyers) may

---

[3] In the gospels of Mark, Matthew and John she is *never* mentioned before the crucifixion.

refer to the same locality. These remarks confirm the town's fishing vocation and the existence of a tower to store fish. The village was sheltered from the south by a beautiful chain of low range mountains, the Arbel cliffs, where a road wound up linking Magdala with other villages in the lake's vicinity, such as Nazareth and Cana. This was the region of the early ministry of Jesus.

**Frans Francken the Younger's painting of the Mary Magdalene washing Jesus's feet**

There is not a single mention in the Old Testament of the town of Magdala, probably because it was an insignificant settlement. Archaeologists have determined that the hamlet began to flourish only at the beginning of the Roman occupation (63 BCE), and it became an important export center. The town was famous enough to have its own stadium, and a small synagogue with interior columns that was discovered in the early 1970s. In 18 CE, the city of Tiberias was built a few kilometers away and replaced Magdala as an administrative center of the region, after which Mary's hometown began a long period of decline, unemployment, and emigration. It is in this context, among rumors of revolts and brigands, that Mary of Magdala heard for the first time the poignant teachings of the man from Nazareth, a moment that would define the early Church.

In search of the historical Jesus, historians are often accused of looking into a well and seeing their own reflection, and thus their own time. Similarly, in searching for Mary Magdalene, novel writers, filmmakers, and spirituality gurus of the last decades have found a liberated woman, a promoter of feminism, a spiritual woman free from male domination, a woman exercising free sexuality, and even the "sacred feminine".

Before the modern era, there was a far different depiction of Mary Magdalene as a repentant sinner who became one of the greatest saints of Christianity, thanks to the forgiveness that was bestowed in abundance by the Christ. That was the Mary Magdalene of the Middle Ages, during which she was depicted as having remarkable beauty and tears in her eyes that signify the insignificant value of physical beauty compared to a life of repentance and asceticism.

*Penitent Mary Magdalene* by Guido Reni

*Penitent Mary Magdalene* by Nicolas Régnier

***Christ and Mary Magdalene*** by **Albert Edelfelt**

Going further back than that, Mary Magdalene was often portrayed as a young prostitute inhabited by seven demons (the seven deadly sins that Jesus expelled from her), the one who wet Jesus's feet with her tears and dried them with her hair. But this is also a composite image, as will be seen below. None of the Gospels identify the woman who anoints and cries at the feet of Jesus as Mary Magdalene, and certainly, none of them labeled her a prostitute or an adulteress.

Thus, underneath that composite is a historical woman of the first generation of Christians, a female apostle, as the canonical gospels hint and the apocryphal gospels (written between the 2nd and 3rd centuries) openly acknowledge. Taking a final step backward, there is only the darkness of Easter Sunday and the figure of a woman standing next to Jesus's empty tomb. About her, the historical Mary Magdalene, it is only known that she was sent to the Twelve with the commission to announce to them, for the first time in history, that imperial brutality and death had not had the last word, and that Jesus had risen.

Aside from the Passion, which consists of Jesus's arrest, crucifixion, and burial, there is only one incontestable mention of Mary Magdalene throughout the New Testament. In it, the Gospel of Luke describes the characteristics of the movement (itinerant), who formed it (the Twelve) and how they obtained their support (sympathizing women). Besides Mary Magdalene, who is at the top of the list for being the most important of "those who ministered," Luke mentions Joanna, Susanna, "and many others." The fact that Luke preserves their names indicates that the three women were prominent in the early years of Christianity, or at least that there was a historical memory of them. "Soon afterwards he went on through cities and villages, proclaiming and bringing the good news of the kingdom of God. The Twelve were with him, as well as some women who had been cured of evil spirits and infirmities: Mary, called Mary Magdalene, from whom seven demons had gone out, and Joanna, the wife of Herod's steward Chuza, and Susanna, and many others, who provided for them out of their resources." (Lk 8:1-3)

To compose his gospel, Luke had access to three older sources: the Gospel of Mark, which he copied abundantly; the so-called Q gospel (which Matthew also consulted), and a special material called "L" by scholars, which is exclusive of Luke's gospel. The mention of Mary Magdalene occurs in "L", unlike other passages (e.g. the multiplication of fish) that appeared in all four gospels. A literary analysis of Luke's text reveals that its author rewrote, edited, and glossed extensively over his material, and this is the case with the passage about "Mary, called Mary Magdalene, from whom seven demons had gone out." Luke assumes that the reader has prior knowledge of the incident and that his audience is familiar with the details, since the healing is mentioned but not described. The gospels were a selection of material that the evangelists had at hand, not necessarily complete. There are other instances in which the evangelists refer to stories whose details they do not give because they do not believe it as necessary, such as when the Gospel of Mark introduces "one named Barabbas ... who had committed murder in the insurrection." Here, Mark assumed that the reader was familiar with that uprising.

Source criticism agrees that Luke's special material predates Luke's own composition, pushing it back to at least the 50s CE, when the first followers of Jesus were still alive. The mention of Mary Magdalene, despite its brevity, reveals three important facts: that she came from the fishing village near the Sea of Galilee called Magdala; that she "ministered" to Jesus (which may mean that she was part of her traveling group, or that she gave financial support or goods to the disciples); and that Jesus cast out seven demons from her. But what does this mean? Although ancient literature saw the reference to seven devils as literal demonic possession, modern anthropology knows that people of the time attributed physical ills (especially those that alienated the person) and mental illnesses, such as hysteria, to demons. The verse indicates that Mary Magdalene was the victim of a number of physical and spiritual ailments, most probably seizures and states of trance. Notably, Jesus was also accused of being possessed several times, a fact that some modern writers interpret as suggesting Jesus performed his exorcisms in a state of trance.

As for the number seven, medieval interpretations wanted to see a reference to the seven deadly sins (that is, Mary Magdalene had every possible vice), but the number seven should rather be understood as fullness, totality, and a total subjugation to physical, spiritual, and social diseases. As in the case of all Jesus's healings, especially exorcisms, Mary Magdalene's true cure was to reintegrate her into her (new) family and into society.

Mark, Matthew, and John keep silent about Mary of Magdala during Jesus´s ministry, but her appearance in the last hours of his life is of extraordinary importance. Many scholars believe that the Passion narrative circulated originally as an independent unit, existing even before the Q source. Some such as Crossan locate their composition in the 30s, a couple of years after Jesus´s death, by the community of Jerusalem. Although it is not clear where the "Cross Gospel" (if there ever was one) began and where it ended - for example, some think that it ended with the burial of Jesus, or, as in Mark, with the discovery of the empty tomb, but before any apparitions - Crossan believes that the original Passion narrative was composed by repetition of the incident by women, those in charge of lament and memory in ancient Mediterranean societies.

In the Passion-Burial-Easter account, Mary Magdalene is heavily involved. Did she have anything to do with the composition of the original narrative? In Mark, the earliest complete known gospel, she appears at the top of a list of women who witnessed the crucifixion from afar. "There were also women looking on afar off, among whom were Mary Magdalene, and Mary the mother of James the Less and of Joses, and Salome (who also, when He was in Galilee, had followed Him and ministered unto Him), and many other women who came up with Him unto Jerusalem." (Mk 15:40-41)

Matthew is literarily dependent on Mark, so he repeats this information, although he replaces Salome for an unnamed woman identified as "the mother of Zebedee's children." Luke, who also was dependent on Mark, has the women "beholding these things", but he saves the apostles´ reputation by adding that "all His acquaintances" were also present. The gospel authors agree that only the women watched where Jesus was laid. John placed Mary Magdalene at the foot of the cross, but he mentions her in passing and instead gives Mary, the mother of Jesus, a more prominent role. Thus, there is complete agreement among all four gospels that Mary Magdalene and other women were present during the crucifixion and were able to watch where the body of Jesus was laid.

In the resurrection narrative, Mary is the central figure. In Mark's gospel, she goes to the sepulcher accompanied by the mother of James[4] and another woman with the purpose of anointing the corpse. Jews used to wrap the body of their dead in various linen blankets and several layers of aromatic spices like myrrh and aloes, after which regular visits to the tomb followed, where the ritual was repeated to make sure that there had not been a premature burial.

---

[4]This woman could be the mother of Jesus, since Mark reports that James was the name of one of his brothers, In other places of the NT, James is well known as "the brother of the Lord."

According to Mark, "And when the Sabbath was past, Mary Magdalene and Mary the mother of James, and Salome bought sweet spices, that they might come and anoint Him. And very early in the morning on the first day of the week, they came unto the sepulcher at the rising of the sun. And they said among themselves, "Who shall roll us away the stone from the door of the sepulcher?" And when they looked, they saw that the stone was rolled away, for it was very large. And entering into the sepulcher, they saw a young man sitting on the right side, clothed in a long white garment; and they were frightened. And he said unto them, "Be not afraid. Ye seek Jesus of Nazareth, who was crucified. He is risen! He is not here. Behold the place where they laid Him. But go your way. Tell His disciples and Peter that He goeth before you into Galilee. There shall ye see Him, as He said unto you." And they went out quickly and fled from the sepulcher, for they trembled and were amazed; neither said they anything to any man, for they were afraid." (Mk. 16:1-8).

**An Eastern Orthodox icon depicting Mary Magdalene holding myrrh**

Mary Magdalene is the first person to discover the empty tomb, and Mark's account makes it appear as though she did not say anything to anyone. It is unclear whether the gospel truly ended in this disconcerting way, without the good news or an apparition of the risen Jesus, or if there was more and the last page of the codex was lost at a very early stage. For example, Biblical scholar N. Clayton Croy believes that both the first and the last page of Mark's gospel were lost. Luke and Matthew, the following gospels in the timeline, both keep Mary's prominent role. In Matthew, women also flee from the empty tomb, but along the way Jesus appears to Mary Magdalene and an unidentified woman also called Mary. Mary Magdalene receives from an angel the news that Jesus has risen, and the exceptional privilege of being the first person to see the risen Jesus.

The Gospel according to Luke confirms that Mary Magdalene (together with a companion) is the first to hear the news from two angels, and the first to communicate the resurrection, but it is Peter who sees Jesus first. (Luke 24:34). The manner in which Luke refers in passing to the appearance to Peter ("The Lord has risen indeed, and hath appeared to Simon!") suggests that there was a narrative of an apparition to Peter that Luke does not know or did not want to include in his gospel.

It is only in the Gospel of John that readers find a complex and enigmatic exchange between Jesus and Mary Magdalene. John, considered by most scholars as an independent source of the synoptic gospels, also knew the tradition of Mary Magdalene in the tomb on Easter morning. She is at the sepulcher weeping because she thinks that the body of her teacher has been taken away when she suddenly sees the risen Christ, making her the first person to experience an apparition, even though she does not initially recognize him. "She turned round and saw Jesus standing there, but she did not know that it was Jesus. Jesus said to her, 'Woman, why are you weeping? For whom are you looking?' Supposing him to be the gardener, she said to him, 'Sir, if you have carried him away, tell me where you have laid him, and I will take him away.' Jesus said to her, 'Mary!' She turned and said to him in Hebrew, 'Rabbouni!' (which means Teacher). Jesus said to her, 'Do not hold on to me, because I have not yet ascended to the Father. But go to my brothers and say to them, "I am ascending to my Father and your Father, to my God and your God."' Mary Magdalene went and announced to the disciples, 'I have seen the Lord.'" (Jn 20:14-18) Thus, in the Gospel of John, Mary is the first person to see Jesus and the first to spread the good news, although, as discussed further below, she is not the first to believe.

Put simply, the four testimonies are contradictory. They don't agree on who was the first to see Jesus, who was the first to learn the news, who was the first to spread the message, or who was the first one to believe, which makes it problematic to try to reconstruct what really happened, or the exact form of the oral tradition from which these four versions derive. That said, all four Gospels have the figure of Mary Magdalene associated with a strange event on Sunday morning at the tomb of Jesus, and all four describe in their own way a supernatural experience (in some cases frightening, in others, dignified and sublime) of the man who had been crucified two days before.

The story of the female followers and the empty tomb sounds authentic insofar as it introduces, from all accounts, three women who have not appeared in the Gospel narrative, only to witness the climactic moment and learn from angels, or Jesus himself, that their Messiah overcame death. It is not Peter, or John, or Pontius Pilate who are there to testify, but a group of unknown female disciples. It is more improbable that Mark and John (the two independent narratives) invented Mary Magdalene (about whom the reader knows nothing), than to accept that this tradition was so firmly established that it was impossible for them to ignore it without risking rejection. That there was a woman of Magdala named Mary who claimed to be present at the founding event of the proto-church is as close to certain as an historical statement can get when it comes to Mary Magdalene.

As for what happened to her after the resurrection, in Acts of the Apostles, Luke mentions that following the physical disappearance of Jesus, the community of believers remained in Jerusalem in prayer. In addition to Mary, the mother of Jesus, she mentions "the women", probably the same women (Mary Magdalene, Joanna, and Susanna) introduced in the middle of his gospel. "Then they returned to Jerusalem from the mount called Olivet, which is near Jerusalem, a Sabbath day's journey away. When they had entered the city, they went to the room upstairs where they were staying, Peter, and John, and James, and Andrew, Philip and Thomas, Bartholomew and Matthew, James son of Alphaeus, and Simon the Zealot, and Judas son of James. All these were constantly devoting themselves to prayer, together with certain women, including Mary the mother of Jesus, as well as his brothers." (Acts 1:12-14).

One last point to consider is the epithet "Mary Magdalene", which may provide a clue about her subsequent work in the Church. The most accepted interpretation is that it indicates her place of birth, but the other possibility is that Magdala (Tower, Great) was a nickname similar to those of other apostles of the inner group. There were at least two other similar cases, the most well-known being that of Simon, the leader of the Twelve, nicknamed Cephas ("the Stone"). Although Magdalene most likely refers to her hometown, the possibility that her nickname denotes her strength in faith, her stature among the apostles, or, as some have suggested, that she wore her hair in a tower-shaped arrangement, should not be dismissed.

From this point forward, the sources of the 1st century are silent about Mary Magdalene, so going any further is entering less firm ground. Before proceeding to non-canonical sources, it is necessary to discard other Biblical stories that supposedly refer to her. From a general understanding, Mary Magdalene was a prostitute, or a repentant sinner, or the romantic interest of Jesus, but none of the gospels suggest this. Three gospels, Mark, Luke, and John, contain the story of a woman who anoints Jesus with an expensive oil that causes indignation among the people present, but Jesus comes out in defense of the woman, exalts her, and justifies her action. Mark and John locate the incident in the town of Bethany, and of the two, only John mentions the name of the woman being Mary, a name that was as common then as it is now. Luke tells a similar story, and taking into account the variation in oral transmission, it is most likely the same incident. The third gospel specifies that the woman was a sinner, and this is what draws criticism towards Jesus. One of the Pharisees thinks, "If this man were a prophet, he would have known who and what kind of woman this is who is touching him —that she is a sinner."

None of the evangelists agree on the identity of the anointing woman, whose story they seem to know only by hearing an oral version of it. It is obvious that by the time they composed their texts, the anecdote had branched into several versions. For John, she was the sister of Lazarus and Martha, a family on the outskirts of Jerusalem. For Luke, she was an unidentified sinner living in Galilee. For Mark, she was an anonymous woman from Bethany who broke into the Pharisee's house where Jesus was staying, and, after her action, she received a surprising distinction, unparalleled in any gospel, or throughout the whole of the New Testament: "Truly, I say to you, wherever the gospel is proclaimed in the whole world, what she has done will be told in memory of her." Who was this woman who deserved such an extraordinary praise from Jesus? Why has her name been lost?

The same can be said of the other figure that has been tied to Mary Magdalene - the woman caught in adultery who is about to be stoned when Jesus intervenes and teaches a lesson to the angry mob. (John 8: 1-11). The narrative places this woman in Jerusalem, and the pericope belongs to a unit that originally was not part of the Gospel of John but instead circulated as an independent piece of tradition. The name of the woman is, again, not mentioned.

If it was possible to apply the same criteria that scholars use on the historical Jesus to determine whether the woman of the Gospels really existed, she would easily pass the criterion of multiple attestation since she appears in at least three mutually independent sources (namely Mark and John, and although Luke is dependent on Mark, his mention of Mary Magdalene derives from Luke's special material). The criterion of embarrassment also works; because the gospel writers had no reason to insert such an embarrassing character in the foundational event of Christianity by recognizing that the original witnesses were a group of sleepy, grief stricken women.

### A Female Leader in the Early Church

Can anything be known with absolute certainty about Mary Magdalene after the resurrection, including her ties (if any) to the Early Church? At the very least, Mary Magdalene must have been an important religious figure for the first and second generation of Christians. Following John Dominic Crossan, one must look at the stories of appearances of the risen Jesus and the people who experienced them as attempts to establish the leadership and authority of one apostle over another, and of one group over another. For the same reasons, there is tension in the narrative over who sat at the table next to Jesus at the Last Supper, who came to the empty tomb first, who saw the risen Jesus first, and who believed in the resurrection first. Paul's case is archetypal when he produces a list of people who saw the risen Christ and includes himself at the end, to insist that his vision was not a simple anecdote but a fact that gave him authority and full status as an apostle. "He was seen by Cephas, then by the twelve, and that He was seen by over five hundred brethren at once, of whom the greater part remain unto this present, but some have fallen asleep. After that He was seen by James, then by all the apostles. And last of all He was seen by me also." (1 Cor 15:5-8a).

The formula had important political implications, shedding light on the controversy over authority and leadership. Paul added, "Am I not free? Am I not an apostle? Have I not seen Jesus our Lord?" (1 Cor 9:1). Notice in this verse the close relationship between being an apostle and seeing the Lord. In other words, in the beginning, the sight of Jesus appeared to confer authority.

Crossan (1994) demonstrates persuasively how stories of apparitions of Jesus to Peter, James, the Twelve, and Paul were not mainly about ecstasy, apparition or revelation, but about authority, power, leadership, and priority. When Paul reminds the Corinthians the names of those who have seen Jesus, he is not putting "emphasis on the risen apparitions of Jesus, but (...) insistence that Paul himself is an apostle, that is, one specifically called and designated by God and Jesus to take a leadership role in the early Church. Despite the admission of belatedness at the end, as well as the insistence on the divine grace, that final sentence put it bluntly: `There is *I*, and there is they, but we are all apostles; I am their equal´. Paul is very interested in equating his own experience of the risen Jesus with that of all others before him." (Crossan, 1994) Thus, stories of apparitions detail the origins of Christian leadership, not the origins of Christian faith.

What then should be made of the firm tradition that Mary Magdalene was the first to discover the empty tomb (according to Mark and Luke) and the first person to see the risen Jesus (according to John and Matthew)? It only stands to reason that Mary Magdalene had a very high authority and preeminence in the early Church, but why wouldn't the New Testament recognize this fact?

Paul may not have included Mary Magdalene in his list of witnesses, but at least by the time of his writing (49-55 CE) women still had the special dignity and consideration that Jesus had granted them. Paul saw them as equals and recognized that men and women had the same rights. In his epistles, readers are told that a certain Priscilla had a church in her house. Another one named Phoebe was responsible for bringing the letter of the same name to the Romans, reading it, explaining it, and interpreting it for them. (Rom 16: 1). No doubt the most controversial instance is a mention of a woman named Junia (Rom. 16: 7), whom Paul calls "prominent among the apostles." Is Junia the irrefutable proof that there were female apostles?[5]

A careful reading of the New Testament reveals a shift in attitude toward women and their gradual displacement from positions of authority. In Paul's pseudepigraphical epistles (written

---

[5] Some interpreters believe that Paul is referring to a man called Junias (a man's name), and some translations of the Bible write it this way. Is Paul referring to a man or a woman? Professor of New Testament Studies Daniel B. Wallace writes: "No instances of Junias as a man's name have surfaced to date in Greek literature, while at least three instances of Junia as a woman's name have appeared in Greek."

after his death, but attributed to him), the author of 1 Timothy wrote at the end of the 1st century or beginning of the 2nd century, "Let a woman learn in silence with full submission. I permit no woman to teach or to have authority over a man; she is to keep silent." (1 Tim 2: 11-12). What is happening here? In the second or third generation of Christians, it is possible to detect a change from a state of equality between men and women (in which both were able to teach and have authority) to inequality, with women being forbidden (at least according to pseudo-Paul) to teach or speak in the assembly.

The final chapters of the Gospels also point to a rivalry between Mary Magdalene (the women in the Church) and the rest of the apostles (men in positions of authority), but this conflict is presented as a parable in the resurrection stories. The Gospel of Mark does not contain stories of apparitions; he has Peter, early in his gospel, as the first one to recognize Jesus as the Messiah (Mark 8:29). However, the evangelist cannot easily get rid of the well-founded tradition of Mary Magdalene as the first person to find the empty tomb and the first to have an experience of the risen Jesus (he details the event in the form of an angelic message to Mary, Biblical language for a mystical experience). The tension is subtle, but it is there. In Mark's telling, Mary Magdalene's revelation is not for her, but for Peter: "Go, tell his disciples and Peter, 'He is going ahead of you into Galilee.'" In the process, he minimizes her role by ending his gospel with the failure of women to give the message - according to Mark, Mary Magdalene and her companions were not able to announce the resurrection because they were terrified.

The Gospel of Matthew, written 10-15 years later, also recognizes Peter's authority (Matt. 16:18) but concedes that Mary Magdalene was the first person to see and worship the risen Jesus, an extraordinary place of privilege. Luke (written around 80 CE) also knows the tradition of Mary Magdalene as the first one to proclaim the *kerygma* (Lk 24:10), but even on Easter Sunday, Luke affirms Peter's supremacy. According to Luke, no one gives credit to the words of Mary Magdalene but Peter, and only Peter runs to the grave, finds it empty, and understands (Lk 24:12). Thus, even though Luke does not know the details, he reminds the reader that the first appearance was for Peter (Lk 24:34).

The Gospel of John composed the final version of his gospel about 10 years after Luke, around 90 CE. Here Mary Magdalene has the highest-ranking distinction, as she is the first to see the risen Jesus, and the first to have a dialogue with him (although Jesus does not allow her to touch him, as he will later grant permission to the apostle Thomas). Mary Magdalene receives from Jesus himself (not an angel) the commission to go and preach (therefore recognizing her authority to teach), but John inserts a curious incident before the meeting between Mary Magdalene and Jesus: "Then Peter and the other disciple set out and went towards the tomb. The two were running together, but the other disciple outran Peter and reached the tomb first. He bent down to look in and saw the linen wrappings lying there, but he did not go in. Then Simon Peter came, following him, and went into the tomb. He saw the linen wrappings lying there, and the cloth that had been on Jesus' head, not lying with the linen wrappings but rolled up in a place by itself. Then the other disciple, who reached the tomb first, also went in, and he saw and believed." (Jn 20:3-8). This brief passage is saturated with apostolic tension, and without a doubt it reflects the controversies between the authority of Peter, the other disciple (John?), and Mary Magdalene, the three protagonists of this scene. Mary Magdalene discovers the open tomb, but it is Peter and the younger disciple who run to check if it is empty. The beloved disciple arrives first, but does not enter. Peter arrives second, but he actually goes inside the tomb, although without understanding what has happened. The beloved disciple, on the other hand, understands and *believes*. He (or she) is the first believer of the Church.

Thus, for the author of the fourth gospel, the real competition was between the beloved disciple and Peter. It is true that Simon ran to the grave when no one believed, and the first one to inspect the empty tomb, the text seems to say, but it was the beloved disciple who arrived first and believed. After all this parabolic competition between the two pillars of the Jerusalem church, Jesus appears to Mary Magdalene, and John recognizes her authority to preach the gospel. The most embarrassing reproach is reserved for "Doubting" Thomas (probably another important leader in the early Church), whom the fourth gospel accuses of not believing the testimony of the apostles and therefore had to be scolded by Jesus himself.[6]

There is nothing innocent in these narratives. Based on the accounts of the gospels, it would be unreasonable to deny that something inexplicable happened on Easter morning, but they were presented more as parable than history. That they have a political purpose is so clear that it is impossible to harmonize the testimonies of Paul, Mark, John and the others. Who saw Jesus? Who failed in the moment of truth and who remained faithful? Who doubted the testimony of the apostles? Who has authority to preach and interpret his message?

No matter the answers to the question, despite the fact the gospels place Mary Magdalene at the tomb, by the 50s CE, there are already signs of a concerted effort to diminish her importance. Already in the canonical gospels, readers can find the beginning of a tension between the Twelve and Mary Magdalene. She was terrified and said nothing, according to Mark. Nobody believed her except Peter, according to Luke. The beloved disciple understood and believed first, before she did, according to John.

The apocryphal gospels, although not a reliable source of information about the historical Jesus, are a good guide to the struggles and conflicts within the Early Church, as well as the various branches of Christianity and their controversies. Scholars like Bart Ehrman have demonstrated that, from the beginning, there was never one form of Christianity, but many varieties. Some apocryphal gospels, though they are useless as a source of biographical information about Mary Magdalene, Thomas, or Peter, are essential to understanding what was

---

[6] Some scholars see here a reckoning between the community of the beloved disciple and the Thomas tradition, and probably a reaction against the teachings of the decidedly gnostic Gospel of Thomas.

happening.

The Gospel of Thomas, one of the apocryphal books containing the oldest traditions, rediscovered in full form only in 1945, is a good case. In verse 114, Peter tells Jesus on behalf of the Twelve, "Simon Peter said to them, 'Mary should leave us, for females are not worthy of life.' Jesus said, 'See, I am going to attract her to make her male so that she too might become a living spirit that resembles you males.'" The authenticity of this saying, which is not canonical, has been intensely debated. If it goes back to the historical Jesus, then he could well be resorting to "enlightened sarcasm" again.

The Gospel of Philip is a document that reached its final form in late 2nd century CE. It was lost for centuries and scholars had only vague reports of it, until it was accidentally discovered in a cave in 1945, in the same codex as the Gospel of Thomas, near Nag Hammadi, Egypt. In its present form, the document is a pastiche of epistles, sayings of the Lord, dialogues and homilies, but it provides important information about the struggle between the followers of Mary Magdalene (and her variety of Christianity) and the male apostles (orthodox Christianity). Philip has preserved the tradition that Mary Magdalene and other women accompanied Jesus. "There were three who always walked with the Lord: Mary, his mother; and her sister; and Mary Magdalene, the one who was called his companion. His sister and his mother and his companion were each a Mary." Mary Magdalene is intentionally left at the end of the list in order to add that she was the "companion" of the Lord. The word Philip uses here is *koinônos*, which means "associated", without a romantic sense.

Later, in the middle of the text, the gospel presents a dialogue between Jesus's disciples regarding Mary Magdalene's preeminence. The evangelist puts such supremacy in symbolic terms saying that Jesus loved her more than others, and used to kiss her, a verse that says more about the rivalries in the early Church than the sentimental state of Jesus. "And the companion of the [...] Mary Magdalene. [... loved] her more than [all] the disciples [and used to] kiss her [often] on her [...]. The rest of [the disciples...] They said to him, "Why do you love her more than all of us?" The Savior answered and said to them, "Why do I not love you like her? When a blind man and one who sees are both together in the darkness, they are no different from one another. When the light comes, then he who sees will see the light, and he who is blind will remain in darkness."

The codex is seriously damaged, so any reading is necessarily a reconstruction. Words in parentheses are educated guesses, and the ellipses are holes in the codex. The paragraph gives a special role to Mary Magdalene inside the church, although it retroactively injects the context of the 2nd century into the ministry of Jesus, a literary technique also used by the synoptic. At the end of the paragraph, Phillip attributes to Mary Magdalene a special spiritual understanding that the other apostles have not yet attained. It is possible that when the author of this gospel wrote this paragraph, it was already a reaction to the gradual disappearance of Mary Magdalene in

Christianity.

The Gospel of Mary, another document of considerable antiquity, was discovered among the merchandise of an antique dealer from Cairo in 1896 and purchased by a German scholar named Karl Reinhardt. It was one of the first Gnostic documents to be recovered after more than 16 centuries. Found in a 5th century codex, most scholars place its composition between 120 and 180 AD. In pure Gnostic style, the Gospel of Mary happened after the resurrection. The apostles are gathered, heartbroken and fearing for their lives, and it is Mary Magdalene who rises and encourages them to fulfill the commission Jesus gave to them: "Go then and preach the gospel of the Kingdom.' Peter stands up and says to Mary Magdalene: 'Sister, we know that the Savior loved you more than all other women. Tell us the words of the Savior that you remember." Then Mary relates a vision of Jesus and launches into an extensive monologue of several pages (most of which are absent from the codex). The narrative part is resumed at the end of the text, where a verbal confrontation between Peter and Mary Magdalene takes place. Peter provokes the rest of the apostles as follows: "Did He (Jesus) really speak privately with a woman and not openly to us? Are we to turn about and all listen to her? Did He prefer her to us?"

Mary complains softly with tears in her eyes due to Peter's lack of confidence. It is another apostle, Levi, who rebukes Simon for his harshness towards the woman. "Then Mary wept and said to Peter: `My brother Peter, what do you think? Do you think that I have thought this up myself in my heart, or that I am lying about the Savior?' Levi answered and said to Peter: `Peter you have always been hot tempered. Now I see you contending against the woman like the adversaries. But if the Savior made her worthy, who are you indeed to reject her? '"

Once they settled their differences, "they began to go forth to proclaim and to preach." The message is that the rest of the churches must recognize that the Mary Magdalene variety of Christianity has a legitimate place among the communities, because its traditions derive from the one person who received a special revelation from Jesus, and it will not be until they are welcomed back to the Church that the message of the Kingdom will spread throughout the Earth.

Mary Magdalene appears in later documents, such as "Pistis Sophia" and others, but they are removed from the life of the apostles and with theological interests too foreign to Judaism and Christianity to be considered of interest, and they do not add new information. However, the Gospel of Philip and the Gospel of Mary uncritically recognize Mary Magdalene´s special status and the attacks she suffered by the other apostles. The Gospel of Mary certainly was composed long after she was dead, but not forgotten. "Speaking" on her behalf, one century or two after she was gone, does not diminish the relevance of the gospel. If anything, it enhances Mary´s importance since it implies that 100 years or so after her death, her name was still thought to carry weight and was invoked to instruct Christian communities.

Taken together, a few historical facts seems certain. In the words of scholar Karen L. King, Mary of Magdala was "a woman, an exemplary disciple, a witness to the ministry of Jesus, a visionary of the glorified Jesus, and someone traditionally in contest with Peter." And most probably, a community of disciples was formed under her name.[7] A century or later after her death, she was still remembered as the Lord's favored one by some communities.

## The Disappearance of Mary Magdalene

Mary Magdalene started the second half of the 1st century CE in a most exalted place among Jesus's inner circle, recognized by some sources as the first person to see the risen Christ, the recipient of a special mystical experience on Easter morning, and an envoy (apostle) to the apostles by divine order, *apostolorum apostola*. Unlike other disciples of the first and second generation (Paul, Peter, James, John, Clement, Barnabas, and others) no writing is attributed to Mary Magdalene, and there is no evidence that she ever wrote anything. As long as no information is available, it can only be speculated whether there was ever a genuine gospel or an Epistle of Mary Magdalene, and if so, how, when, or why it was suppressed. Unless there is a new archaeological find, it's likely safest to assume no such writing ever existed.[8]

In the 2nd century CE, Mary Magdalene enjoyed enormous prestige in some Christian circles, and she was considered to have had a more intimate relationship with Jesus. But from then on, the historical Mary Magdalene began to coalesce with other women in the gospels, such as the adulterous woman and the sinner weeping at the feet of Jesus.

In 591 CE, Pope Gregory I - the last "good Pope" according to John Calvin - picked up on a tradition that had already developed and determined the fate of Mary Magdalene for the following centuries: "She whom Luke calls the sinful woman, whom John calls Mary, we believe to be the Mary from whom seven devils were ejected according to Mark. What did these seven devils signify, if not all the vices? It is clear, that the woman previously used the unguent to perfume her flesh in forbidden acts. What she therefore displayed more scandalously, she was now offering to God in a more praiseworthy manner. She had coveted with earthly eyes, but now through penitence these are consumed with tears. She displayed her hair to set off her face, but now her hair dries her tears. She had spoken proud things with her mouth, but in kissing the Lord's feet, she now planted her mouth on the Redeemer's feet. For every delight, therefore, she had had in herself, she now immolated herself."

The apostle from Magdala was thus officially immolated in the Western Church, possessed by demons, reputed to be a prostitute, and no longer recognized as the recipient of a special revelation. She was only seen as a female follower in need of forgiveness. "Across time, this

---

[7] The apostle Paul complains for the division in the Church in communities loyal to one or another disciple: "It has been reported to me by Chloe's people that there are quarrels among you, my brothers and sisters. What I mean is that each of you says, 'I belong to Paul', or 'I belong to Apollos', or 'I belong to Cephas', or 'I belong to Christ.' Has Christ been divided? Was Paul crucified for you? Or were you baptized in the name of Paul?" (1 Cor 1:11-13)

[8] There have been several attempts to demonstrate that the Gospel of John was actually written by a woman, the beloved disciple, namely Mary Magdalene. The name "John" was attached to the document later, and it remains strictly anonymous.

Mary went from being an important disciple whose superior status depended on the confidence Jesus himself had invested in her, to a repentant whore whose status depended on the erotic charge of her history and the misery of her stricken conscience" (Burstein, 2006). In other words, Mary Magdalene was portrayed as the redeemed whore of Christianity.

Within Judaism, Mary Magdalene was also vilified. The Talmud, mistaking her for Jesus's mother, says that she was "Miriam, who let her hair grow long and was called Stada (adulterous). Pumbedita says about her: `She was unfaithful to her husband.'"

Of course, the need for a female figure in Christianity did not vanish, and this need came to be satisfied by another Mary, a much more harmless female follower, one who had never competed against any apostle: Miriam of Nazareth, better known as the mother of Jesus. It is interesting to note the strong contrast between both figures, particularly the belief in Mary Magdalene being a prostitute and Jesus's mother being a virgin. Susan Haskins (1995) supports the idea that the cult of the Virgin Mary, a phenomenon owed to the Syrian church in the 4th century CE, merged Mary of Nazareth with Mary of Magdala, and even asserts there was "a deliberate and systematic superimposition" of the two later in the history of the church. In the 2nd and 3rd centuries, the apocryphal gospels spent time discussing the biology of Jesus' mother, to the point of bad taste (whether or not her hymen was broken when her son was born, or whether her other children "opened her belly"), and the Orthodox Church was confident to advertise her as an example of a virtuous and eternally virgin woman. By the end of the 3rd century, the first prayer to the Virgin Mary appeared, and in the 4th century churches began to be dedicated in her honor, notably in Ephesus, where a famous council would take place. In the 5th century, a specific Marian liturgical system was established and the Council of Ephesus proclaimed her "Theotokos," a Greek word meaning "Mother of God."

In medieval times, Mary Magdalene was subjected to all kinds of legends. One of them said that, after the ascension of Jesus, she lived for 30 years in the desert, without food, assisted by angels. In later legends, Mary Magdalene was said to belong to the nobility of Jerusalem and to own many goods. She retained her status as a sinner, and did it for pleasure and not out of necessity. One of the most interesting and most enduring legends claimed that Mary Magdalene (along with her brothers Martha and Lazarus) was put on a fragile boat by the people of Egypt who opposed the Christian message. The boat arrived on the shores of Marseille, one of the most prosperous ports of the Roman Empire, now part of France. Together with her siblings, Mary Magdalene evangelized in that region of Gaul, one of the first places where Christianity actually took roots in that part of the Mediterranean. Later, she became acquainted with the king of Marseilles after miraculously healing his wife and son. A newly discovered panel attributed to Erhard Altdorfer (16th century) shows that the cult of Mary Magdalene was significant in that country. The second part of the painting displays an apparition of Mary Magdalene during the Battle of Bornhöved in 1227. The female saint looks identical to the Virgin Mary —standing above the clouds, shining cloak and hands in prayer position— except for her bright red hair.

During the Middle Ages and Renaissance, Mary Magdalene would remain a blonde or a redheaded woman, depictions that were pointed out by an increasingly anti-feminist clergy as characteristic of public women. Blonde was, as today, considered exotic and desirable, but censured. "During the Middle Ages women continued to dye their hair blonde, despite exhortations to the contrary by clerics, who pointed to the blonde tresses of the temptress Eve (perhaps thereby making blonde hair even more attractive). For the Europeans of this period, blonde hair represented dangerous eroticism, sexual temptation, and beauty." (Trask, 2003).

From then until now, new approaches came up. Every year, historians come up with new theories about one of the most controversial women in the Bible. One of the most resonant works in popular culture placed Mary Magdalene as the wife of Jesus and mother of his children. According to Mario Arturo Iannaccone, a historian of Christianity, the idea that Mary Magdalene was the lover of Jesus was born in the Parisian "counterculture" at the end of the 19th century. "For example, in 1888, an opera titled *The Lover of Christ* was performed in Paris," he explained in an interview with journalist Massimo Polidoro. "It was written by Darzens, and the lover was, obviously, Mary Magdalene. In various novels, Mary Magdalene became a *femme fatale*. Lawrence, author of *Lady Chatterley's Lover*, wrote a story about Mary Magdalene and Jesus titled *The Risen*, filled with double meanings."

In *Jesus Christ Superstar*, a rock opera released in 1970, the Christian Messiah was presented to the counterculture generation of the 1960s alongside a conflated Mary Magdalene, a "free lover" who wipes Jesus´s feet and sings "I don't know how to love him." Just a few years ago, novelist Dan Brown based one of the 21st century's most famous books on the old conspiracy theory that the Catholic Church had covered up the marriage of Jesus and Mary Magdalene (and their offspring).[9] In 2012, a documentary by journalist and filmmaker Simcha Jacobovici claimed to have found the sepulcher of Jesus's family. The tomb of the Christian Messiah, he asserted, laid alongside that of Mary Magdalene and their children. Scholars quickly dismissed the film as misguided and manipulated. The same year a fragmentary text of the 4th or 5th century written in Coptic came to light, quickly dubbed as the "Gospel of the Wife of Jesus" after a line that read, "Jesus said to them, 'My wife ...'" and then the sentence breaks off. Perhaps not surprisingly, recent research revealed the so-called gospel to be a modern forgery.

Without question, the fascination surrounding Mary Magdalene will continue, and new "discoveries" will be made and published, but the furor and sales generated by her enigmatic figure will not change the fact that there is very little anyone can truly know about her. As a historical person, Mary Magdalene leaves the pages of history after Easter Sunday. Nobody can know what happened to her after the proclamation of the "tribe" of the Christians began. Mary Magdalene was probably a respected authority among the Christians of Jerusalem from 30-60

---

[9] *The Da Vinci Code* sold 80 million copies. Not many have realised that the novel took the basic postulates from a book called "Holy Blood, Holy Grail", which proposed nothing new either. There seems to be no end to novels, comic books and documentaries about Jesus´ wife and children.

CE, prestige derived from the fact that she was the first, or one of the first, to have a vision of Jesus. It also seems probable she was opposed by the Twelve, admittedly because she taught things that seemed foreign to them, and therefore was excluded from the inner circle from the beginning. She is never mentioned in Acts of the Apostles, Luke's text about the history of the first decades of the Church, and while Acts doesn't hide the fact there were disagreements between the apostles, it never mentions Mary Magdalene among those present at the first council of Jerusalem in 50 CE. (Acts 15).

It is possible that Mary Magdalene was received by the family of Jesus (her mother and the beloved disciple), and that her testimony was vital to the composition of the fourth gospel, which places her in a more exalted place. Raymond Brown, a prominent biblical scholar, suggested that the Gnostic Christians emerged from the Johannine community (and hence from Mary Magdalene's teachings), and that they produced the documents that exalt their figure over the other apostles (Gospel of Philip, Gospel of Thomas, Pistis Sophia, Gospel of Mary, etc.) at a time when the historical Mary Magdalene was only a distant memory. The Eastern Church holds the tradition that she died in Ephesus, present day Turkey.

The discovery of the "Gospel of Mary" at the end of the 19th century revived interest in her, but it has been used for diverse causes, from female liberation to New Age proselytism. The historical Mary Magdalene was, ironically, subjugated once again to modern sensibilities, now in the form of a liberated woman, representative of the "sacred feminine", Jesus's wife or lover, and/or the initiator of a sacred and real dynasty. Either way, her face has again been obscured and her voice silenced, as it was in antiquity. In the same vein, the abolition of her authority and apostolic character was a major point of departure in the withdrawal of women as apostles in the early Church, with negative consequences for the great Christian denominations, which blocked their ordination until recently. In 1977, the Episcopal Church ordered its first woman, and 1990 brought the first female Anglican minister. It was not until 2014 that the Anglicans approved their ascent as diocesan bishops. To date, the Catholic Church —the oldest existing branch of Christianity— has not opened priesthood to women.

In order to be faithful to Mary Magdalene's memory, one must go back once again to that dark Easter morning, beside the tomb of an executed prophet, where the other women and Mary Magdalene experienced something so strange that they "were terrified", an encounter so difficult to describe that their words were considered as irrational tales by the Twelve. Mary Magdalene is a figure whom the evangelists would hardly introduce had she not existed, one whom Paul, defending the historical reality of the resurrection, had good reasons to avoid. The Gnostic documents contain many pages of teachings attributed to Mary, but they were written centuries after her death, when everyone who had known her was long dead. In the end, the woman of Magdala left us with one single sentence, the only words attributed to her in the entire New Testament: "I have seen the Lord." (Jn 20:18).

At the very least, it is a line very few people in the Bible could say.[10]

**Online Resources**

Other books about Christianity by Charles River Editors on Amazon

Other books about Mary Magdalene on Amazon

**Bibliography**

Bauman, Richard A. (1992). *Women And Politics In Ancient Rome.* London: Routledge.

Burstein, Dan. (2006) *Secrets of Mary Magdalene.* CDS Books

Crossan, John. (1994) *Jesus, a Revolutionary Biography.* Harper San Francisco.

Haskins, Susan. (1995) *Mary Magdalen: Myth and Metaphor.* Riverhead Trade.

King, Karen L. (2003) *The Gospel of Mary of Magdala.* Polebridge Press.

Polidoro, Massimo. *In Search of Mary Magdalene*, Skeptical Inquirer Magazine, March-April 2016.

Pomeroy, Sarah (1994). *Goddesses, Whores, Wives, and Slaves: Women in Classical*

Starr, Lee Anna. (1955) *The Bible Status of Woman.* Zarephath, N.J.: Pillar of Fire.

Tetlow, Elisabeth M. (1980) *The Status of Women in Greek, Roman and Jewish Society, in Women and Ministry in the New Testament.* Paulist Press.

Trask, H. A. Scott, *Blondes Through the Ages.* American Renaissance Magazine, August 2003.

Vázquez-Lozano, Gustavo (2016). *The Apocryphal Gospels.* USA: Charles River Editors.

---

[10] John also puts these words in her mouth: "They have taken away the Lord out of the tomb, and we know not where they have laid him", a redactional sentence invented by the author who was presuming what she might have said on such occasion.

## Free Books by Charles River Editors

We have brand new titles available for free most days of the week. To see which of our titles are currently free, click on this link.

## Discounted Books by Charles River Editors

We have titles at a discount price of just 99 cents everyday. To see which of our titles are currently 99 cents, click on this link.

Made in the USA
Lexington, KY
27 February 2018